To Mary —
midwife to many of these
poems.
I look forward to seeing
a copy of YOUR book.
Love,

Scenes From My Trip

Poems 1998—2010

Annette Hollander

Full Court Press
Englewood Cliffs, New Jersey

First Edition

Copyright © 2010 by Annette Hollander

Published in the United States of America
by Full Court Press, 601 Palisade Avenue
Englewood Cliffs, NJ 07632

ISBN 978-0-9846113-0-0
Library of Congress Control No. 2010931263

Editing and Book Design by Barry Sheinkopf for Bookshapers
(www.bookshapers.com)

Cover photograph by the author

Author photograph by Sri Walpola

Colophon by Liz Sedlack

DEDICATION

This book is offered in gratitude to all those who offered inspiration, encouragement, and critique, from poets Jill Bialosky, Ana Doina, Marie Ponsot, and especially Diana Festa and the Madison Poets, to friends such as Diane Churchill, Jane Goldsmith, Jane Isenberg and Michael Laikin. And to my family: Myron Kaplan, who has the first poem, Amelia Kaplan, who once had a Poem-a-Day, and Eve Kaplan-Walbrecht, who writes her own, thank you for having been, and being here with me.

Table of Contents

1

I

A Note Of Gratitude
To My Husband

You built the scaffold of my life
Architect, engineer and general contractor
Framing is solid, lines clean, no leaks
Everything works the way we intended
I had the good sense to hire you
I am the envy of all my friends

THE GROWING SEASON

Those
seeds stuck
to red ground
wet from the rain.
We sweated, planting.
I remember the day
so well, holes for the seedlings
under blue sky. It was June, late
for our area but we figured
it didn't matter; late food is still food.
Farmers want to be first to get the best price.
We had enough time before the first frost coming,
Green dots made miraculous lines, seedlings made blossoms.
After we tried to hoe the weeds we bought a big machine.
Everything was leafy. It was so hard to tell what was what
(except for tomatoes.) One day I saw a bud on the zinnias,
sunflowers leaping up. That week each day was sunny, ninety.
I saved the crop hauling water in red gasoline cans.
Corn was especially thirsty, and the peppers, too.
Rabbits ate sweet peas, and flea beetles arugula.
We couldn't pick zucchini or cucumbers
fast enough to keep them from becoming
monstrous. Some we sold, some gave away.
Eggplant hung purple; tomatoes green.
Then, suddenly, we couldn't
find enough zucchini.
But wasn't it just
yesterday we
put those seeds
in red
dirt?

ROSE GARDEN

My roses have heart: brave buddies!
Look at them, tall and skinny, hanging over February snow,
refusing to drop their leaves
even when asleep.
Load them with ice now,
they'll still bud out when the forsythia blooms.
That plant you think dead
will sprout canes strong as whips.
Cut each bush harshly —
they like that; they get stronger,
giving me buckets of flowers in season.
The more I take, the more they give.
Tiny green aphids suck their juice; fungus invades—
they survive; what spirit!
They give me the strength to come back
year after year.

The In-Between

I am dormant
Caught in the gap
Between life and new life

Something looms
Will the world end
Or sprout?

Cold silence
Is my answer
It is quiet here

Mostly peaceful
A little longing
A little hunger

Waiting for sap to flow...
It's not true
that if we don't grow, we die

We know
when the time is right
to break out

RUNNER IN EARLY SPRING

Mansions in all stages of rising or falling,
a yellow door, a purple garage.
Billowing tarp on an old Victorian with crumbling columns,
sidewalk cracked into angled slabs like the Appalachian Trail,
and mulch, everywhere mulch.
One crocus.

In the park, an overflowing stream undermines the road,
magnolia blossoms hide in their buds.
White cat bounds across the road.
A man with a buzz saw chops twigs.

Decay and renewal run through my town—

In my headphones
a robin sings
to Beethoven.

Spring Cheating

Spring says it's coming,
but don't believe it.
Disaster, not daffodils
can come at any time.
Don't imagine roses
because one cardinal sang this morning,
be prepared—
no power, no water.
Those swelling buds:
Charlatans!
Impostors!
Nature's con artists!
Mud and rain will continue
interrupted by snow,
my inner landscape
wind-blown steppes of Central Asia.

Don't tell me about sun, or grass
until my dreams come true.
Nothing to rejoice about,
except that the fallen tree
landed on the roof
gently.
Get it? Now go away
And leave the cave-bear to sulk.
She won't come out
Until it's the real thing.

DO NOT DISTURB

Listen, Spring
I'm not ready for your advances—
plant your green kisses on someone else,
stir their passion with warm winds,
fragrance from melting ground.
I don't want to burst
like the red maple buds
outside my window.
Please, I need to think clearly
to finish winter projects you
drive out of my mind
with each dawn chorus.

But I am no virgin;
I know what will happen—
I will yield, one more time,
to your shameless promises.

THE REAL TWO WEEKS

Daffodils are opening at the bottom of the hill,
little light bulbs.
Do I see green in the lawn? Do I hear it?
Pea-sized swellings on bare twigs:
will they be leaves, or flowers?
I have been waiting for months but it is still too soon.
I see tiny white rosettes of the first weed,
and spikes of dandelions to come.
Spring's cart wheels, stuck in the mud,
finally pushed off down the mountain;
beauty is rolling now out of control:
magnolias, tulips.
I want to slow it .
"This is the real two weeks of spring," my daughter said,
and I thought. . .
What about lilacs? Apple blossoms?
Rainbows of irises?
But she is right.
These are the real two weeks of spring,
welcome, terrifying.
This is the real shock of redemption.

Beauty Contest Of The Blossoms

Flowering Plum and Magnolia say,
"We are the first to wear new clothes
so we dazzle,
the rest of you still naked."
Cherry says,
"I am the ballerina of trees,
graceful in the wind."
But Crabapple says,
"None of you can match my colour;
I am sunset
In the middle of the day."

In My Rose Garden

Second week of May

An elegance of buds
split crimson
peek from sepals.

First week of June

Too soon, petals of striped Scentsation
litter smooth grass;
Sunsprite gapes open;
Dolly Parton's orange bosom
looks like a cabbage.
Black Spot invades Garden Party
and even Pristine unfurls.
In my rose garden, I work
to erase imperfection
so we can live in paradise again.

FIREFLIES

I

Lust, flying slowly, flashes
Desire blinks from the bushes
Brilliant points of longing
perching on their blades of grass
or drawing light-lines in the dusk
weave a serious conversation

II

Why does their glitter comfort me
watching in the drowse of evening?
They're only beetles, looking for a mate
So? Stars are only burning gas
These little ones are living light

III

Hey! Little lust-lights who brighten my life
Thank you for drifting with your belly lanterns
looking for love on my lawn, or in
shadowy bushes where she sits,
sparkling

Summer Solstice

Where I live, light wins by five.
We play life in bright rooms,
or alleys with shadows.
In the short dark we drum,
dance with bare feet.

Flute music spangles the morning;
vines on the hillside wrestle toward the light.
Ancient oaks look young again.

I want to take you
where twilight slides into dawn,
drink wine with strawberries,
gaze at the river.

July Swimming

A cripple enters green water—
miraculous cure!

                              Never the same—
                              like sunsets or sex

The sun
is under my armpit

SUMMERHOUSE BY THE SOUND

Returning to where we all began,
I enter green water.
Overhead, eye-scalding blue,
underfoot, translucent pebbles on ochre sand
meet the sea's shifting skycolor.
On the bluff, peach and crimson daylilies
preen, speckled with Queen-Anne's Lace.

Sunset's epic poem brings orange,
new verses every evening,
a violet curtain when the story is done
and the audience retires, satisfied.
Fog or night may hide this,
but every year, winter will erase it.

No one is allowed to stay
in paradise.

Autumn Accounting

It's up to you
to count the leaves
that will fall
tumbling down
the mountains

If you call yourself
aware
neglect none
not the oak leaf
with wormholes
or the crackled maple

In a storm you will
find yourself challenged
testing your powers
as the trees
divest

But the path
to enlightenment leads
from the first red sumac drifting lazily
to the last beech leaf

Pay attention

Like God

In Autumn I Ride My Bicycle

Over a parallel universe
of leaves like lemon drops.
Milk chocolate great oaks stand tall.
Japanese maples sprinkle cherry candy;
Sassafrass can't quite make up its mind
between lime and orange.
Someone has been decorating the cake of the world:
on top, my purple bicycle.

The Day After

Yesterday the leaves peaked
which in this part of the world
means eruptions of brilliance.

Trees are supposed to be green,
not the color of cardinals and goldenrod.
Maybe today is the peak,
or tomorrow?
An occasional skeleton of a tree says otherwise.

Yellow and brown postcards
drift toward me
saying, "It was a good trip, wasn't it?"

How can I not be sad
in this season where beauty comes
from endings?

Poem In The Chinese Manner

Late autumn wind—a monkey screams—
sneaks through cracks in my house.

Outside, the North Star guides seamen
over black waves.

The rose bush, fragrant last summer,
now— stumps eaten by deer
whose tracks sink in wet sand.

FIRST FROST

Last night at twenty-nine degrees
the autumn garden became detritus,
bloom to waste in twelve hours.
Blackened like gangrene,
yesterday's dahlia stems droop,
without substance,
without turgor.
Soggy spent blossoms show
no color.
Leaves melt.
Cold had no teeth
until ice snapped cell walls.
Knowing this would happen
can not stem
grief.

WINTER LIGHT

glints off parked cars and through swamp weed.
Leaves scurry like mice.
A lone pine scrubs purple bellies of clouds;
other trees drawn in pencil.
Long shadows at noon
signify
the coming dark.
Along the river, wave tips like silver fish
shine,
briefly luminous.

Winter Geometry Lesson

Parallelograms of trees
Vines, loopy parabolas
Rock cubes line the stream
Covered by jagged rectangles of ice
White planes of snow
And everywhere fractals, fractals, fractals

WINTER SOLSTICE
"The thing is what it is, not what we call it."

A time when the Earth, fleeing the sun, gets caught
and is pulled back

        OR

You could say when Earth, yearning for the distant sun,
has finally accepted loss of love

        OR

You could say that our Earth, watching its distant love,
sees it turn,
arms outstretched.

WALKING IN LATE WINTER

Nothing moves except me
Sap sits underground
Oaks have no leaves to flutter
Brook, shut down with ice
Even soccer ball rests
on dry grass

But our sun
drifting toward the mountains
already plans
a party

2

It Happens

Racing to the underwear airport
suitcase unpacked, purse stolen
unprepared for the math examination—
toss, cursed dreamer. Flee those assassins.
Let your parrot escape through your car window;
she'll freeze, but you'll live to dream again.
Kill your husband, or have someone else do it
violently, with knives. Hide, under the bed,
as the thundering asteroid punctures your ceiling.
The end is near, tonight, and again tomorrow.

GRANDMOTHER RAP
(after listening to a poetry slam at the Nuyorican Poet's Café)

Hear that big guy
with glistening black skin
complain that everyone stereotypes him?
See the pretty blonde tossing her fur
complaining everyone stereotypes her?
No sympathy from me.
I'm totally
INVISIBLE

I can outrun you, sweet.
Why do you offer me a seat?
And why are you so perplexed
that I mind being unsexed?
A woman with lines in her face
can't possibly be writing love poems to a man—
It's a disgrace!
But maybe it's an allegory about Time, or God.
That wouldn't be so odd.
Give me a break.
I know, it's unnatural I make love better than I bake.

The young poet cried, "Can you see the ocean that is in me?"
Sure. Can you see my Caribbean, my Mediterranean sea?
Don't stereotype me and I won't stereotype you as a callow
youth,
well meaning but shallow,
gritty as a marshmallow.
That's all you are, you know it
when you only see your mother in me, not another poet.

So parents have a hard time seeing their children as real people,
and children feel queasy about Mommy and Daddy having sex.
I know this is the way.
But I'm not your Mommy—
you didn't grow up having to do what I say.

I'm envious of your energy. I'm impressed.
You're building the house I will live in. I'll be your guest.
But poems don't age much. Sappho still creates a sensation.
All you need is a good translation.

Let's shoot a zipline across the generation gap.
What's the matter, you never heard GRANDMA RAP?

The Alzheimer Patient Writes a Poem

Keep it simple
Nice, clean words
Out of my ears
Into the ground
Who knows
What's needed dear
Are you listening
Time was
To make music
Carry on
Do you sing
Lovely
To show your leg
Even in school
Do what I tell you
Never mind
Never mind

Yoga Class

Ribs open like gates
Ready for light and sound to enter
Navels curve like an ear
Toes feel their way
Toward a place to stand
So many ways to be in the world
Inverted or twisted
Lying as if dead
Fold into gravity or rise above
Stay where you are and be strong
Breathe
Mind follows

POETRY IS FREE

Glory hallelujah!
Paintings cost money
and good paintings cost a lot of money
A trendy sculpture can cost more than your house
Many books and magazines discuss
the latest fluctuations
in the price of art
but poetry is free

Poems are free
you can copy them out in your own hand
for the price of the paper, and your labor
Better yet, memorize them
brain cells are free, too
Why buy a book of poems?
You can borrow from a friend
Imagine hoarding poetry:
Come to my house
A great poem is locked in my vault
No one has seen it for a hundred years
since the author died and her daughter sold it
and it's mine! All mine!
Imagine lines around the block to hear a poetry collection
gathered from around the world
Awesome! This may be your only chance
to know these works before they go back
to museums, in countries you will never visit
I would love to see a contemporary poetry auction:
the house packed; bidders on the telephone
as each poem is given a price

Thank goodness poems are free
Pass them out on street corners
No one will get rich reselling them
except in pleasure
Only libraries have to buy the books
to give poets their daily bread
Maybe that's why in our country
there's no respect for poets
who have to live by teaching
or serving cappuccino

In Iceland

All is sex.
Rifts where Earth quivered and split
streak the grassy hills.
The geyser spurts: "I am Earth's ejaculate."
Moss, alpine flowers cling to black lava chunks.
Life is peaceful now,
if you don't look too deep.
Water reflects sky in craters where the mountain
exploded.
Sheep graze. People swim in steamy pools.
This "solid" ground is a crimson flow
that has cooled
but presses, bulging.
Only Gaia's thin skin keeps us from burning alive.
The fumarole instructs:
 "Look into Earth's lava-womb where it all began."

RIVERSIDE PARK, NEW YORK CITY

Thin sticks of fence
keep dogs and vandals away from cherry trees—
blossoms fluffing overhead like cotton candy—
fencing out you and me.

We cannot immerse ourselves
in this lake of petals—
only watch
April's motion picture.

"Look but don't touch" makes me sad.
At our nature center, kids cannot leave the trail—
too many people,
too little nature.

We are creative with barriers—
use telephoto lenses to get close.
But I would rather, like a deer, leap that little fence
and eat my fill of blossoms.

After 9/11—New York City

When disaster comes to visit our town
and moves right in with us, we cannot say
"Go home!" This is his home now, and we must
get used to having smoke-filled breath around.
Whether we go across or up or down
town, disaster follows. He won't go away.
We cannot force this bad guest to leave us.
At night we wait for unexpected sounds.

Candles and memorials surround
grass in the park where children used to play
neighborhood games. Who knows who we can trust
or if the wind is safe to breathe? Stay down.
Disaster creeps into our bed at night,
grins, "Pleasant dreams," and then turns out the light.

DARK AGE
(September 11, 2001)

Here come the barbarians
speaking their brutal tongue
come to kill us

swarming over the hill
like black ants
from all directions

staring with dark eyes
indifferent to statues
and marble baths

toppling our towers
retreating to caves
ending our pleasures

We could bring them
running water
civilization

They don't want
our indoor plumbing
They are barbarians

Even armor
cannot protect our legions
who want to live

Seasons At Flat Rock Brook: Haiku

I
Tiny violets
  hiding beside the cold trail. . .
  They know it's spring.

Wild red-bud blossoms:
What tame tree could equal them?
Not cherry, not plum!

2
Jump in the pond, frog;
Run away, rabbits and snakes.
Your people are here.

3
Four year old hiker
picks up seven yellow leaves
shaped like his hand.

Five year old hiker:
stoops to pat shelf fungus,
ignoring the rain.

4
Snow powders blue ice
pressing on dark pond water,
on sleeping turtles.

And one more Haiku for Mercer, Gallya,
and the Flat Rock Brook Gardeners:

So much hard labor
to make it look natural. . .
wildflower meadow.

CRESCENT MOON

What's new under the moon?
No real light leaves this curved
sliver of lemon rind,
but still it became blazoned on flags,
dragged across battlefields,
as did two shapes of star.

A country should adopt
a blade of grass
for its flag.
That would be new.
On the battlefield,
grass always wins
sprouting green and proud.

Down On The Farm, Or Sonnet To The Dish

Great ring of metal, like a gaping mouth
Sucking in the glory of the sun
Sits on our farmhouse rooftop, facing south,
Dwarfing the house. It's possible someone
Might find it pretty, if they didn't miss
The old days when we talked to neighbors, friends,
Instead of staying in our rooms like this,
Watching the flickering light its signal sends.

Once we used to look at stars and moon,
But now there's so much more for us to see.
The spheres are singing news, or a cartoon.
It scoops up these vibrations silently,
Throwing its black shadow on the snow.
Come on in, stranger, and we'll watch a show.

HER HONOR

Blind Justice sits with her chin in her hand,
legs crossed, thinking.
When she tries to move,
her black robe trips her.

In the courtroom, big bellies and gaunt faces
debate, gesticulating.
Impassive backsides
feel the edges of chairs.

The cast of characters includes usual suspects:
a fat cat sweating in his waistcoat,
bored cop with a pistol, an Indian.
I swear I tell the truth!

Crossing this clean, airy room: webs
of slander, bright lights, nightmares.
Our case unfolds as snails climb Mount Fuji—
slowly, slowly.

They speak of "miscarriage of justice"
as if she were pregnant. That could happen today:
blood streaming down her robes.
It was false labor. We are sent home to wait.

The deciding moment stretches into years.

How difficult to be enlightened
by the knowledge we are One—
when I am innocent and he is guilty.

METAMORPHOSIS

In Greek, *amphíbios* means two lives,
not counting the angelic egg—

tadpole to hopping frog
from silky water to wet land.

Other animals get second rounds;
caterpillars on the parsley grow butterfly wings—

whose grub are we?
I want metamorphosis.

It is time for something new, but natural—
and I don't mean Death.

We think our next stage is "spiritual", disembodied.
That is a failure of imagination:

It would be fun—perhaps change the world—
if everyone had a chance to be both sexes.

Give us nerves that wince
when someone else feels pain;

then we could not make war.
We might become human.

SCHUBERT PIANO TRIO # 1

I sigh with the viola for all the world's poor
who cannot be here with a full stomach,
enjoying piano's champagne.

I know they are me and I am them,
and yet music's sweetness
can not feed them.

I am helpless,
frustrated,
charmed with harmony.

A new plague approaches from the East
as this movement of the trio
ends.

SURFING THE STOCK MARKET

RICH   Ride the spiky wave,
POOR   go under, pop up.
            Toes in the sand,
            race back into foam.

RICH   Thrill as the crest runs,
            brings you along
POOR   smashes you
            on the beach

            where you dry off,
            rest in the sun,
            then paddle lazily
            turn, try again,

RICH   surf's roar in your ears,
            one with its power
POOR   until you swallow brine
            grab mouthfuls of air.

            Wave follows wave.
            Will the next one
            lift
            or destroy you?

Back To Eden

Nobody thought the end would come so fast
although we all had grim imaginings.
I, personally, was afraid of things that flied
in the night and bit, their tiny kiss
filling your blood with microscopic death.
That wasn't it. Some frightened themselves with
visions of conflagrations, fires of war,
blinding lights and radioactive ash-
which happened once, but then we tamed that beast,
and we survived. When we began to fill
both air and oceans with the excrement
of the same machines that let us live so well
some thought our own cells, growing uncontrolled
(just like ourselves) would kill us in the end.
That happened to quite a few, but I survived.
Others looked into the future, saw
the ice caps melting, flooding cities, but I,
admitting that would be a nuisance, knew
mere floods would never spell the end for us,
survivors of the Ice Age. I was right.
But having been right is hardly comfort now
that I'm alone, and everybody's gone.
My parents had to feel this when they watched
their parents die, and then their friends
and all their cousins, funerals every day
because they lived to overripe old age.

Hardly anyone dreamed the end would come
in tempting shapes of apples, golden wheat,
potatoes bred to poison insect foes.
Delicious food, immune to mold and worms,
coincidentally would paralyze
our little sperm, which lived, but could not swim.
And so my generation is the last,
but apples never have been shinier.

MONEY

Not paper, not metal, but power
Imagined safety

No toddler tantrums when you can't have the candy
Grab the candy, trainloads of it

Bury playground bullies with a hostile takeover
Or hire bodyguards

No more pre-teen shame about pimples
Buy respect in other ways

No more teenage angst about guilt
Give your money away

And in old age, dream about
Making your children happy after you're dead

But lose it, and you are four years old again
Looking at people's knees in the elevator

Do I Know You?

At the reception, can you find the poet?
Some are disguised
as suburban mothers, ingenues,
little old ladies in lace collars.
Women with angelic faces
write of war, of exile;
others, wrinkled, sing passion.
That black guy you're scared of—
the one with a skull on his biceps—
has published and
the dark-eyed Jewish boy your mother wanted you to date
displays his homosexual affairs
in little magazines.
Now and then a poet will look the way they're supposed to—
Irish, with wild hair.
I am having some difficulty sorting this out
because the little old lady
also shows photos of her grandchildren
and I saw the black guy
hanging out on a street corner.
Where is the badge saying
"Bearer of wisdom, of pleasure"?
A secret society with a secret handshake?
No luck.
I will just have to assume everyone is a poet
although some have to dig through miles of rock
to find soul's groundwater.

3

SOME QUESTIONS

How many love poems are enough?
Can there be too many?
Imagine 8 billion humans on our planet
millions in love
of these, thousands writing poems
to cool their throat
to woo the beloved
because they have to
Do they litter the noosphere with their poems?
How many ways can be found to offer one's soul?
As many as Nature finds
to shape a leaf?
What of the other millions:
rejected lovers complaining—
how can we recycle their laments?
Where do they go? Into compost and ocean?
Should there be a limit?
How many love poems are enough?
As many as we see paintings
of the crucified body of God?

There And Back Again

Let go. Push off. Travel. Take free time.
Broaden my mind until it grasps the world.
Sharpen it on mountains. Make the same
effort to know strangers and taste weather.
Bite off delightful details, as the whole
reveals itself bit by bit, hour by hour.

My first trip: I will not forget the hour
I spent fleeing that Algerian, an endless time;
police were watching us. That taught a whole
lifetime's worth of facts about the world:
I kicked him and he ran. . . I recall weather
teaching Art History, sunsets the same

orange as Van Gogh's sunflowers, same
genius touch portraying the first hour
of dawn. American or Dutch, the weather
hangs on museum walls, where every time
I see a painting, eyes reflect a world
existing somewhere, pieces of the whole.

So many pieces in this puzzle, whole
continents of roofs and rivers, same
scanning eyes. And do I know the world
now that I've smelled tarred roads hour after hour?
Antarctic fields that never know springtime
are only tiny lessons about weather.

Keep walking till I get away from weather.
In Asia will I understand the whole?
There's never enough money, enough time.
London, Lourdes, Lhasa— not the same.
How can I close my eyes, when any hour
I might just see that one place in the world

that lets me know I now have seen the world?
It's late, and once again uncertain weather
fools me, and the last train left an hour
ago. Do I have a hotel? This whole
enterprise somehow is not the same
as when I started out, eager that time.

World, you have seen me. Now I sing the whole
way home, love our own weather, want the same
old friends, talking for hours, time after time.

THE COMPUTER PROGRAM

says, "Press Enter"
to wake the screen from darkness—
one touch.
Take my hand
press any key. . .

The Hungry Poet

The hungry poet forages for words.
They hang just past her reach on lofty trees,
on mountainsides.
She digs for them with a dull digging stick.
Thick roots are stuck
in dried-up soil. She isn't getting much.
Starvation looms,
but ever hopeful, she keeps moving on.
Around the bend might be
more luscious fruit.

Ode To Orchids

How you contradict yourselves!
Thick-fleshed, beefy,
with delicate

ruffled petals: Cleopatra's
jewelry, royal purple, garnet
luring the moth.

"Come and eat!"
your fragrance announces,
even when there's no food.

Treacherous beauty!
Butterflies searching for love,
cheated by false wings in red and gold,

withdraw smeared with pollen,
to implant on
other orchids.

Bees need long tongues
to slurp nectar hidden deep
inside the labellum—

Other plants bloom at the same time each year.
You bloom when you want to,
if you want to.

A sheath appears, holding the ripening
flower, which may unfold in months,
or this week.

You don't need soil,
just a bit of bark to grasp
while sipping from the cloud forest.

What kind of plant
throws roots into the air,
heedless?

More species than beetles,
more colors than stained glass,
I want to give thanks—

You bring creation's
strange game
into my living room.

SKIN RIDDLES

Riddle: Where is the miracle?
Answer: With us, every day.

We walk around for years feeling whole
while our container regenerates.
Living boundaries
keeping the world out,
can erupt, ooze hot springs,
flake away like dead leaves,
thrill us with pleasure.

Riddle: This package dies if unwrapped.
Answer: You and me.

FATHER'S DAY

Under white flowers
and lime-green leaves,
the tree trunk stands
hidden in shadow,
easy to overlook,
supporting
its family of blossoms.

Create images the shape of nothing.

Speak of love and horror. "I like being scared", says little Forest, monsters and dinosaurs his friends. "Befriend your beasts", said the Mind-doctor, wisdom-pusher. Accept it all. And I did, for one proud moment. Help create a new reality with more love and soaring. Only parasites I can never accept. That is the test.

Everything is in the intervals, if you know how to listen. In the breath's pause, in hunger pangs. In word combinations:

"The backbreaking effort of night"
"Day's slippery escape"
"Chained by logic"

Speech is the key to making people do what you want. Is it bad that Maia learned "Triangle"? Will it limit her imagination, or will she build cities with triangles?

Filthy rich with words: "Hippopotamus". "Avocado".
"The cherry jam of good judgment"
"Lemonade of able listening"

See me walking the deck obsessively looking for a flashing light.
"Triumph of clouds"
"Skitter of bats"
"Frenzy of children"

"Coagulate" is a good word, if you're not in the mood to fly. Wild associations purge the pores, clean out nostrils, purify crevices and moist places.

Why stand in my way? Let me go on and on, won't you, while I finish my knitting, wait for the bus? I am just creating my own adjective world.

THE WILD ANIMAL SPEAKS:

I circled you for a long time
You drew me close
I waited for a false move
You made none
When I snarled or cowered
You stroked my fur
Now I can be still when I am near you
They call this "gentling"

What The Stream Had To Say

What the stream had to say was: Don't worry
Light that breaks up comes together again downstream
When something blocks you, go over, under, around it
Be sure to giggle the whole time
The stream says: Life is

What the stream had to say was: I know you
I've been in your body
Do you sense me? Mud, roots, and waterfall
insect and birdsong, moss and fern?
Droplets?

What the stream had to say was: I'll tell you
anything you want to hear
I speak all languages
I let you be part of my flow
Now cool your feet

Untitled

Most of the universe is space
Sitting across from you I see
where I could fit into the gaps
between your atoms
There's a place
inside your sweetest skin for me
after all distances collapse

LOOKING

I am looking for a poem
on the New Jersey Turnpike
Could I have left it at your house?
Hawks are practicing their penmanship overhead
Flocks of swallows make inkblots in the sky
Patchwork leaves are piled by the side of the road
Have you ever tried to find a poem in a leafstack?

My poem could be hiding
under the covers of evening
or imprisoned in a dragnet
with sad dolphins undersea

Perhaps I will have to go on a Quest
climb a glass mountain to make myself worthy
and grab the enchanted binoculars
before I can claim the Poem

By the side of the highway
flag-waving reeds grow tall enough to hide in
but my little poem
could be at home
under piles of old photographs
I will keep looking

Digital Love

Scan my image
Make it bits
Make it pixels
Turn grey to brown
Put in highlights
Take out shadows
Maybe even add
More people
Or take me as I am

MAKING A MEADOW

One year we plow, spread wildflower seeds—
gold poppies, purple larkspur—
they bloom, a backdrop
for the dance of first love.

The next spring, stiff hands push
up through the sandy soil,
honey locusts' insinuating fingers,
offspring of the silver trees that ring this acre.
I remember when that forest, too, was open field.

I renew my vigilance—
go out with my crusader's loppers in August
to waste the infidels in their prime
but I tire and they grow thicker.

Honey locusts have thorns.
They grow so fast,
they are the first to fall
in hurricanes.

Now only among pebbles up on the hilltop
where young trees won't sprout
do a few clumps of fine grass wave
like a proper meadow.

We could plow again, but that's no victory;
That just returns us to the beginning.
Must I give up my vision
of two teenagers chasing each other
through wild flowers?

TROPICAL WINTER SOLSTICE

Florida sunshine soothes,
warm waves dissolve tight bodies,
but dreams know
life is at its
low ebb.
Royal palms sway green
around contented golfers
but thin bones sense
early darkness
even here
in the land of lollipops.

McFaddens Pond

I know how you feel
every time a leaf falls on your skin,
then slowly drowns.

Visitors stop to rest,
gaze at last year's leaves
under reflected clouds.

Mud furrows your face.
Cattails grow
where sunfish played.

Once you were broad, deep and blue,
wavelets kissed by the wind
slipping over the dam.

Now every storm brings debris,
chases your water out,
turns blue to brown.

But peeping frogs breed here;
you still are Home—
Blue herons stay by your side.

On The New Jersey Turnpike

My mind
Fog on asphalt
Dried-up leaves
Clinging to their trees
My thoughts

But the road
Wide and flat
Reassures
It must lead
Somewhere
I can follow

SWIMMING MEDITATION
OR, DO FISH EAT BUTTERFLIES

I slip into warm water, become
a pink seal gliding through green space.
Ahead lies a drowned butterfly.
My breath slides in and out.
Why won't fish eat the butterfly?
One rock, then two, pass by.
White seaweed strokes my arm.
In front of me, killifish streak,
won't be caught.

When the seal tires, I roll on my back
and the great current of our moon's pull carries me home.

God Comes To Me At 6 P.M.

God comes to me at 6 P.M. That's when
brick walls begin to glow, when golden light
flows down old theatre posters and graffiti
beckon, awesome. See my city shine!
People in busy streets carry their glow
on pinstripe suits, not knowing they are blessed.

I do nothing to deserve my being blessed
an hour before sunset. Even when
dark thoughts pollute, silences can glow.
Familiar dirty avenues delight,
sport elevated subway cars that shine,
decorated with the best graffiti.

I'm not a person who would make graffiti
or spend much time thinking about being blessed;
I'm always stunned when streets begin to shine,
sidewalks implode. I can't believe it when
I feel that Presence in the spreading light.
I stare, not seeing my own body's glow.

Once I saw fields and a farmhouse glow
(initials cut in bark are trees' graffiti)
Watching the hedgerow in the evening light
-even barbed wire fences can be blessed-
I could not say what happened to me when
I was only eight and saw the shine

the first time, sitting down, feeling the shine
embrace the meadow while the skyclouds glow
surrounded ponies. Blackbirds, flocking, when
the sky grew red, drew lines of wild graffiti.
I never thought, then, about words like "blessed;"
I only knew I was part of the light

that quivered everywhere. This moving light,
fifty years later, strikes me with its shine
abruptly as the first day I was blessed
with losing me. I hope you've seen this glow
even if you've never heard graffiti
say, "Now!" Open your eyes. I told you when.

And in that hour of glow, when flaming light
shines on our world, on cow dung or graffiti,
anyone, anywhere who sees it can be blessed.

REALITY

Wet sand
when I pick up a lump to examine
crumbles
grains slip through my fingers
no more lump

Electrons
tell us their position or velocity
not both
and they construct our reality
No wonder you're so elusive

You,
when I think I know you,
disappear
reappear in front of me
smiling

I
slink through spacetime
uncertain
of my position
and my speed

EATING IN THE STREET

Walking down the street, running my tongue
over folds of chocolate ice cream cone
or licking the drip off sticky fingers
I wonder, am I offending someone?

I put French fries in my mouth, one by one.
Why, in some countries, is this taboo?
I understand privacy for sex,
but I want the world for my dining room.

THREE CHEERS FOR THE SILVER MEDALIST

On Vesuvius, we reach the grass-rimmed edge of one crater
but are locked away from the peak
by uniformed guards
closing the gate
so we cannot hike up those gritty paths
like pencil lines drawn in black dust
to where the great cone towers,
cannot stare into its hell-hole, or dominate
the circle of the world.

But we can stand here where the old mountain blew,
pluck golden scotch broom from volcanic ash,
lean transfixed against a railing
as the sun drowns between misty islands,
and lights sparkle the city
below.

Though our bodies never stood on top of the world,
gasping from the climb,
I have seen postcards.
Sitting at home again, does it matter
that I never really trembled in awe
at smoke twirling up from invisible depths,
never sat and toyed with
sharp stones?

MEDITATE ON THE VOID

The void will come to you if you open your chest,
now filled with old shoes and party dresses.
Do you want the Void to come?
Do you have a choice?
Who's at the door?
No one, no thing.
You forgot to send the invitations.

Things are real once you decide that's so.
The party rages all around. Wine helps.
So many pretty people, all you, you know.
And music descends like snowfall
from the band playing at the top of the stairs.

Quiet within! Someone cries.
Destiny enters, carrying gifts.
You are happy to see her—
Everyone wants to feel part of the warp and weft of things.
What a party!
Too bad it has to end.

THE RUNAWAY UNIVERSE—A TRUE STORY

Our universe is running away—did you know?—
away from YOU. Our space is stretching out.
In several billion years, our sun, that burned
so bright, so long, will shudder and expire.
What you thought to call empty space is filled;
that space is pulsing with dark energy

(called dark because we don't know what it is)
pushing and shoving heavenly bodies apart.
All galaxies move swiftly from each other.
Everything, even our milky way
flinches from everything else, and all the suns
burn down, cool off, never to be reborn.

You know what this means? One bang, not many.
And the cosmological constant is less than one
but more than zero, and that means no rebirth -
only a long dying, or, you could say, long life.
Once born, but only once. So we are like
the universe; there is no second chance.

You Know Who You Are

As my mother the fortuneteller
used to say,
you are outwardly confident,
inwardly shy.
Good-looking,
perhaps not so sure about that.
Under your knowing smile
lurk many questions.
Your past holds a secret
you would not like your spouse to know
and as for your future—
money will come and go again,
children, too.
You will take a trip
and stay in good health
until the unexpected
strikes.

4

In The Womb

Let me out of here, I'm restless.
I want to stretch.
There's nothing to look at and nothing to think about.
I can be poisoned, or bumped.
This isn't all it's cracked up to be
by some weary people.
Sure, it's great not to be hungry,
but I'm looking forward to tastes.
This has been fine for a few months—
but I don't think I'll want to come back.

CHILDHOOD IN 1946

The Fluoroscope

You went into a shoe store, where you put
your shoes inside this weird machine. You saw
your feet inside your shoes. You saw each bone
inside your feet, glowing green as ghosts.
You didn't know, then, that to see through toes
could kill you. You had fun, and no idea
that these same rays might slightly rearrange
the molecules that make you who you are.

The Wall

I loved to pick at the paint on my wall-
peeling paint, little cracks, pink and grey.
As I lay by the side of my bed
I would carefully pull it away
from the wall, and then stick out my tongue;
I tasted each flake for a while
then crushed it to bits with my thumb.

I hoped Mom would never find out.
Do you remember that too?
The sweet taste of plaster dust
and the hole in the wall when you're through.

My New York, My Forest

On Park Avenue where there is no park,
only fenced-in grass parting downtown from uptown traffic,
someone added cherry trees when I wasn't looking;
in spring they drop real blossoms.

My childhood friend
was a tree I named Rag Mop
for the rag wind-wrapped around a branch.
I thought it was called a sycamore
because the splotchy bark looked sick.
It's gone—now Chinese Gingko
sprinkles a little shade in the summer.
I don't know when that changed.

On my mother's Fifth Avenue terrace
we planted a mountain ash
that tossed its yellow leaves in autumn
like a zoo leopard, pacing.
That terrace crumbled into the apartment below.

At Christmastime,
fragrant evergreens for sale
lean against walls, rootless.

But on 96th Street, children still pull
at the chains of swings,
feel themselves flying into ancient elms.
All year long on the sidewalk
little cages protect
tree trunks
skinny as a leg.

THE THERAPIST'S CHILDHOOD

Everyone's childhood becomes mine:
Joan, fondled by her teenage brother Steve
while she lay in bed, age five,
wonders if Steve remembers.
Later, he called her "loser," while Mom and Dad laughed.

If I had a brother, what would he call me?
Maggie's brother is one of her best friends.
She raised him, while Mom smoked cigarettes,
afraid to leave the house.

I never asked my mother for the name
of my own brother, stillborn nine years before me.
She grieved for him every year and I was angry.
Even when I imagine him I hate him.
He would have played catch with our Dad.
He would have gone to medical school instead of me.
He would have had his pick of girls.
What's-Your-Name, stay underground!

But the twin sister I never had
was good company at night in our bedroom.
She understood me.
Though we laughed at the same jokes,
she was no help at Dad's funeral,
or in Mom's last, crazy years.
What's-Your-Name, I wished you had been there.

TOWN MEETING

The community of selves has a town meeting
Some are more outspoken than others
Who holds the real power?
The well-dressed one with smooth hair and black boots
or the the child huddled in a corner?
When you need consensus
the nay-sayer controls

The issue is: Can we trust this man not to hurt us?
Can we trust anybody not to hurt us?
Someone points out it's a little late to be having this discussion
Someone else has evidence: happy memories, a poem
years of faithfulness
The child begins to cry. She is hungry
Someone has a banana. She eats it

The Buddhist quotes the First Noble Truth
which is: "Life hurts, get used to it"
and the Second Noble Truth
which is: "The cause of that hurt is human need"
Someone sighs, "So what do we do?"
The meeting adjourns with nothing solved
but everyone feels better after getting together

SLEEPAWAY CAMP

Brown-haired Melissa, sad-eyed, dumpy child,
where are you now? When you were eight, at camp
and far from home, I was your counselor.
You couldn't swim, you always missed the ball,
you weren't pretty like the other girls.
Your Mom wanted you to lose some weight
and be someone she could feel proud of.

I took you to the lake's edge every day.
You lay in shallow water, terrified.
I held my hand under your rigid back;
soon you relaxed, your belly riding high.
I lightened my touch each time, until one day
I didn't touch you and you didn't sink!
You loved to float, now, looking at the clouds.
Next year, maybe, you would learn to swim.

Inside our bunk, one rainy afternoon,
desperate for ways to pass the time,
I dragged out e.e. cummings and showed my girls
ways poetry could look, and sound, and feel.
Jane wrote: "I like to play, all night and day"
Melissa wrote about our overnight:

"Last night the moon shone bright in the sky
I run, run, but there's no use
The moon is still in back of me

Slowly
        the
                moon
                        disisappears
                        and
                                the
                                        sun
                                                comes
                                                        out"

Visiting day. Melissa ran to Mom
"I learned to float! And I'm a poet! See!"
"That's nice," her mother said. "But can you swim?"

MOTHERHOOD

Mothers are always wrong.
My mother was,
and hers before that.
It's in the DNA.
They are selfish creatures,
doing what they want
when they should be making our favorite food,
playing games with us,
holding us close.
Everybody knows that Daddies have to work,
but mother's job is to keep us satisfied
and if we're not
we know
where the fault lies. . .

CRAZY GLUE

Sex is the glue
Crazy glue
Bonding life to life
Keeping contact
Without it we split apart
Or fall off
With one touch of this
We hold together

Outside The Airplane Window

My chair and I hover 35,000 feet above ground.
Angels once lived here—
now only a blue-white mist spreads above the field of clouds.
We have flown into the regions of God's majestic abode
and found
Ozone.
Where does God live now?
We have looked into the spaces between atoms
and seen
Electrons.

But there is always a Beyond.
My mind pushes at this fence,
never glimpsing the other seven dimensions
of our universe—
only the old familiar four.
God could live there
or between these lines
or inside our brains—
even outside
the airplane window.

LYING IN THE CEMETERY ALIVE

Lying in the cemetery alive
on the ground
on my back
on the close-cropped grass

watching white clouds pass
over head
over stones
over the family

grieving for all our dead
under drifts
of cloud
in a summer sky

Lying in the cemetery alive
over bones
over cropped grass
with open eyes

Waiting for understanding

REMEMBERING DREAMS

Last night's dream
If only I could remember
Such elegance
Such drama
Something about chariots
Or was it staircases
Where are the details
Lost in a swamp
My childhood
And how you smelled
Last Friday
Smiles and hollers
So many chapters
Written
Unwritten
So much vapor
Drifting over the sidewalk
So many kittens
Becoming cats

SHREDDER

Time is a wastebasket.
I reach in to rescue a memory;
the pieces are neatly sliced,
indistinguishable.
You say:
"How can you not remember
the name of the man
who loved you
while you tortured him?"
I only see the hilltop where he watched me paint.
You say
you know the color of the carpet
in your childhood home.
My carpet has been shredded.
When my wastebasket is full,
will I be empty?
I grab blank paper and make new memories
as fast as I can.

MOTHER DEATH

waits for us, knitting.
She sits up late at night
waiting for you to come home.
Please, Mother, be patient
while we play out our lives.

You With Fear Of Dying

I do not dread dying
Every night I slip away
from this life
so I know how it is
I dread each winter's dying of the light
Two and a half minutes a day
Walls of my room closing in
Water in the pail
Freezing
Death is not like that
Dying is a respite
from our well-known selves
A long vacation
Somewhere we have never been

CLIMBING THE HOURGLASS

Does the sand really run faster
as it gets near the end
or does it merely seem so?
Am I rehearsing for a happy day
that will pass faster than the rehearsal?

The more I try to move into now's eternity
the more seasons stream past.
This afternoon green buds pop,
yesterday I was shoveling snow.
Shortly after tiny leaves
have filled the sky,
they will shrivel.

Scrambling in the hourglass,
I can't stop sliding,
want sticky finger-and-toe pads
that would holdfast on glass.
I don't want to climb back up,
just stop falling, falling

This is my favorite time of year—
so much anticipation: my birthday,
filling the pantry in the summer house,
swimming—
and then all will have come and gone.

The breeze is soft on my cheek,
I like writing poems.
It's not that I'm not enjoying
This moment—

really, I am—
but my desire to grasp it,
almost spoils the pleasure.

Suddenly I stop trying,
find myself here
where there is no dread
and no swimming just yet
but there are daffodils
and my children
laughing
and fighting.

THEY SAY

You can't go back
be the baby you never were
well fed
contented
held and petted
They say just mourn it

You can't go back
they say
but they never really tried to find out
never made the leap

You can go back
I know
It is never too late
to sink into bliss
smile and clap your hands

They say you can't go back
but I know plenty of people
who say they've been born again
into one kind of love or another

5

HAPPY POEM

Today the clouds with their little grey bellies
shine brightly against the October sky
And the tree-of-the-day contest winner
blazes out of control, and my dahlias grow high
And the squirrel in the middle of the road
looks me fully in the eye
And both my children are almost in love
And no one is sick or about to die
And I checked "excellent health" at the clinic
So today I am happy and all that is why

MATURITY

A hawk
used to be
my totem animal
Soaring king of the skies
surveying
the curve of the world
No fear, just hunger
Riding updrafts
like a ski tow along the cliffs
Gliding down invisible trails
Days of that
Never tiring
And when the chill came, moving south
That was the life I wanted

But now—
I am an overfed Persian cat
See me, on my favorite sofa
in that streak of sunshine
sitting on a pillow
immobile
If I move
I stalk my food bowl
My people caress me when I ask
otherwise leave me meditate in peace

The hawk outside my window
shrieks for dinner

To Sharon

One moment everyone in the family rallies,
shielding your brave body from cancer
with anything at our disposal:
shopping bags and telephone calls.
Grabbing brooms and bedpans,
we work as a team in relay, never yielding an inch.
Suddenly, everything changes;
you moan, and you won't stop moaning.
We put away our stuff.
"Come on in," we say to Death. "Have something to eat."

UNVEILING

(In Memoriam—Sharon Kaplan, 1917-1999)

The grave looks lovely
although they couldn't keep you in it.
Nodding blue and yellow pansies,
newly planted, cheer the mourners,

but you're not under them.
You were needed elsewhere,
comforting someone, giving perfume or watches,
and most of all, advice. . .

The headstone looks lovely
and so do your children and grandchildren
who feel sad
and crack jokes.

You came back today to take a look
to make sure everyone's doing it right.
And we are, because we knew
you would be here to supervise.

ALL CEMETERIES ARE THE SAME

All cemeteries are the same:
blocks of granite
on grassy expanses
dotted with trees
like a savannah.
Hawks circle lazily looking for mice;
crows roost.

And the words on the tombstones:
beloved,
wife, husband, mother,
born here, died there.
Sunlight the same,
and shadows.

Never the same—
our minds when we visit
or the lives
we strain to remember.

ARRANGEMENTS

(an epithalamion for Eve and Chris)

In Victorian times, the gift of a flower or a bouquet
carried a message, since all flowers have a meaning

Starry cosmos, sunflowers studded with bees,
multicolor zinnias that keep coming,
you bring in bundles from your farm.
How will we arrange them at the wedding?

You want the guests to do it.
What if they compose by meaning?
Spicy yellow buttons of Calendula
say "Joy" in the language of flowers.
Sweet Basil, "Give me your good wishes."
Zinnias: "Thoughts of absent friends—"
lovely meanings, an odd bouquet.
Asters spell "Love," but Sunflowers, "Pride,"
Snapdragons, "Presumption. . ."
All thrive in late summer soil.

No one will have seen such a wedding
with guests selecting,
clipping and tying stems,
filling containers with water,
while your orchestration
makes harmony
with colors and shapes
arranged by different people.

You like challenges, you two,
meet them with energy and improvisation,
create the life you want.
Guests will remember
how you grew the arrangements—
no two tables the same—
flowers from your field
speaking their blessings.

FOR MORRIE

I keep telling friends
what a kindly death you died:
age 87, still driving,
still hitting the ball.
No months of nurses turning you in bed.
No years of children visiting whose names you forgot.
No endless days of pain or nausea or tubes.
I tell them how grateful we are
for that chance to say goodbye
so we don't have to feel guilty
for aggravating you the month before.
I tell them how you would have hated
the life of an invalid,
how you were always too proud to ask for help,
how this kind death protected you from shame,
the "fate worse than death."
They nod in agreement, but we also agree
no death is kind to us,
forsaken,
left behind.

To Newborn Forest

Welcome, little lump of potential
Pure being and becoming
With kicks and grimaces
Cuddly as a puppy
Soft and strong
Already with talent—
To suck and grab
And stir tenderness in all who see you

In Memoriam: Robert Krudop
(1938-2003)

I.

I saw you wrestling with an angel.
I want to go home, you said.
The angel was solid, strong like you,
with hair on his arms.
You were beginning to fade around the edges,
which gave the angel an advantage.
You glanced at the heavenly host
waiting to welcome you
(and outnumbering you)
but kept struggling.
I have to go home, you said.
There are Christmas trees to plant and others to cut,
stone walls to build and drywall to tear down,
grandchildren to cuddle and scold,
bucks to hunt.
My wife is recovering from surgery—
we haven't seen our Caribbean home in three years.
I love Jesus but I love her too.
My children turn to me for advice, for support.
I don't want to be here;
I want to be with them.
The angel pinned you.
I began to see through you.
The angel said, "You can't go back
You don't have a body any more."

2.

(For Bob)

How can a man who is larger than life be dead,
without ever being smaller than life, weak, feeble?
A man like the boats you loved,
laughing when you made a sharp turn,
throwing up spray, making us scream.
A man like an SUV, working in all weather,
undaunted by hurricanes or snow.
A man like a truck,
going all day on one tank of prime rib,
like an eighteen wheeler, hard to budge.
A man like a Cadillac, reliable but fast,
with the biggest engine in town
racing down the road.
How can your motor be dead
and none of us able to fix it?

Waiting For Forest

June 11

Souls are quarreling to enter my daughter's body,
eager to try again in this fractious world.

I dreamed great battles between good and evil,
one night one wins, one night the other.

You have no idea, the shouting, the shoving
(metaphorical, or course, without bodies)

and Eve goes about her business, a week past due;
nothing can happen until this is decided.

June 12

Rosebud daily pinks up, swelling,
opens sepals to become rose,
but the baby whose spine I just saw on the ultrasound
must be squeezed through a tunnel
too narrow for his bones,
in danger of losing life support.
No wonder he won't leave.

June 17

Birthing is a teacher
about our limitations.
Watching waves stripe the horizon
or the sun's egg crack into the water
we learn how things happen.

This child, unborn but visible
will open his door in his time.
We can only wait to welcome him
With milk and kisses.

FOREST 19 MONTHS

Pick up
Put down
Check it out
Turn it around
Throw it away
Give it to me
Put in your mouth
Or bring it to E

For Shira

(age 2½)

Sing a song of Shira
Pockets full of play
Make us giggle with you
Make us go away

Sure of yourself since a toddler
Busy with your stuff
You love to make us laugh
Tell us when you've had enough

Cuddly but assertive
Serious and gay
I know you, little sweetheart,
Your mother was that way

FOR AMELIA AND MOI

In your marriage I foresee
not blending, but twining,
not like a Pollock—
spots of you, flecks of me;
not like fudge—
you're the chocolate,
I'm the cream,
but like your logo,
a new design,
something lovely never seen before—
Amelia and Moi, Aleph and Mem distinct,
intertwining vines growing toward each other.

Waiting For Two Babies

I want to see them:
Ears, eyelashes, raspberry mouth.
But is she breathing, is he fully human?
Changelings lurk behind the drapes,
Midwives not to be trusted.

Two babies, two chances for joy or grief,
And fate's graffiti is unreadable.
I cannot decipher it or look away.
Everything grows on this spring afternoon.
Will you be clever, will you be kind?

My unborn muse,
What cute things will you say?
How will you break my heart?
My mind wraps around you,
A receiving blanket.

Are you deformed, ghastly, hideous?
Say the unthinkable
Nature can be cruel.
I promise to love you, little beings
No matter who you are.

A Shakespearean Sonnet For Maia Shani

I could love your fair skin, such perfect peach,
Or choose your eyebrows, arching above eyes
Pure blue, or say how little fingers reach
Into my heart. It comes as no surprise
That every sound you make alerts my brain.
I run to you at your least little cry
Because I want to know you feel serene.
And when you let me take you in my arms
I feel so blessed I could walk on air.
Many, like me, will melt before your charms.
Sweet Goddesses all listened to my prayer.
But with all this, it is your lips, God knows
That hypnotize me: petals of the rose.

TO NEWBORN RAFAEL ASLEEP IN MY ARMS

You had better grow up
To be a little angel
Because your parents
Named you Rafael.
Sleeping here, tiny eyelids closed,
You could be,
But I am full
Of questions:

What will you want to be
On Halloween?
Whose genes are busy
Expressing themselves?
Your redheaded sister
Loves to pat your silky black hair.
But will your eyes stay blue?
So far you have been mellow
About joining our world—
Few screams of protest,
Mostly "More milk, please."
How long will that last?
Among all the questions,
I know one thing my angel—
You have blessed us,
We will guard you.

About the Author

Annette Hollander wanted to write a book before she was forty, and so wrote *How To Help Your Child Have a Spiritual Life*, which was published in 1980 with a paperback edition in 1982. Poetry didn't count—that's what you wrote for yourself.

After starting to write poetry more seriously in 1998, she sent out a few for publication and got some published in little magazines. When the *Journal of the American Medical Association* (circulation 180,000) accepted a poem in 2004, she stopped sending them to magazines—that was enough.

But then the poems also wanted to be in a book.

Annette Hollander's day job has been (and still is) psychiatrist and teacher of psychotherapy, mother, and now grandmother.

This book has been set in Hoefler's *Requiem*, derived from a set of inscriptional capitals appearing in Ludovico Vicentino degli Arrighi's 1523 writing manual, *Il Modo de Temparere le Penne*.

Breinigsville, PA USA
27 July 2010
242542BV00001B/12/P